How to Write Your Book 101

Everyone has a book in them!

Adebola Adisa

CONTENTS

Page Blank Intentionally

Dedication

For Adetola Adekunle, my sister and friend.

Through thick and thin.

May you always have joy, peace, and love.

Acknowledgment

My utmost gratitude goes to God, as I am fully aware of how much He has blessed me.

I have the best family and the most gracious friends.

I will always be grateful to my loving and dependable parents Anne Olusike Adekunle and Olasupo Olutunde Adekunle.

I am thankful for my supportive husband Adeniran Adisa. I love you.

To Orinayo and Mo, my forever blessings, what a privilege to be your mum.

Thank you to all my siblings, Adesola, Adeniyi, Adekola, Adetola and Adebiyi.

To my friend like a sister Rita Shoremi, you and the 'crew' mean the world to me.

Thank you to my editor Sarindar Kaurah and John Williams at London Logo Designs.

To everyone in my life, past, present, and future, thank you all.

About the Author

Dr Adebola Adisa is a wife, mum, GP, inspirational speaker, and author of four books. Adebola is also a school Governor, STEM Ambassador and PRO of the Black Women in Health (BWIH) a group for diverse black women in medicine and healthcare.

She is the founder of Brave Hearts North East CIC, in the North East of England. The group support their community and promote holistic health through sports, health talks and participation in the yearly Race for Life event organised by Cancer Research UK (CRUK).

They also raise funds for their local NHS Trust Charity, the County Durham and Darlington NHS Trust Charity and have recently launched a mentorship program for secondary school pupils in Darlington.

Adebola promotes healthy living through articles; health topics, poetry and other inspirational writing on her social media pages and is the face of the NHS England #helpustohelpyou campaign.

She stays active by walking and running and enjoys spending time with her family, cooking and exploring new dishes. She believes that everyone has a book in them and is passionate about assisting them on their journey to writing it! Her life motto is #beinspired.

Page Blank Intentionally

"Everyone has a book in them. You have a book in you. Write it"

- Adebola Adisa

My tongue is the pen of a skilful writer.
Psalm 45:1 (CSB)

Do You Dream of Becoming a Writer?

Have you been struggling to write?

Do you see yourself as a writer?

Are you hoping to publish your book?

If you answered yes to any or all these questions, this book is for you!

Read on and see how "*How to Write your Book 101: Everyone has a book in them!*" will help you become a better writer.

1. I wrote this book in 30 days

Yes, you read that right. It took me only 30 days.

This is proof that anyone can do it.

If you are motivated enough, you will find time to write your book.

2. Simple jargon-free language

I have written this book in plain language. There is no fuss, airs of sophistication or peculiar terms requiring a dictionary to explain.

You can read it at your leisure as you follow my personal stories and writing experiences.

3. Concise

a. You can read through it in a few hours and still feel the sense of achievement that one gets from completing a book from the front cover to the back page. One thing that limits or prevents us from reading is the sheer volume of many books. You want the closure to say, 'I completed this or that book'. At the same time, it shouldn't feel as though you are studying a textbook for schoolwork.

I have experienced the same, thus I aim to pass the core message in as few pages as possible.

b. Time-efficient self-help book

This book is a self-help book which provides basic, yet adequate writing tips which will allow you to start writing your book immediately. I have equally considered how precious your time is.

c. Reference

You can go back to read again and again or refer to this book each time you seem to be stuck during your writing.

Becoming a Writer

Poetry was my first literary love. Unquestionably, it still holds a very special place in my heart. I once wrote an essay in primary school, titled "Myself". The essay was about who I was, my family, my favourite things and what I would like to be when I grew up. I wanted to become a 'Farmacist' like my dad. I guess ending up as a medical doctor is as close as it gets!

Consequently, in secondary school, I wrote poetry across a variety of topics, love, friendship, hope, heartbreak, and the uncertainties in life. While in medical school I had joined the press club. Here I did some amateur journalism and event reporting, which in turn improved my writing. However, I still ended up writing more poetry.

I have never stopped writing poetry! I have written several poems starting from my teenage years and now have a moderate poetry collection. If you ask me to choose two of the favourite poems I wrote, they are "Life's Good" and "This Season for this Reason".

The poem, "Life's Good," reads like a song. It speaks about the treasure and sanctity of life and encourages everyone to preserve, nurture, celebrate and care for it.

On the other hand, the poem, "This Season, for this Reason", reiterates the true meaning of Christmas and what we really ought to celebrate.

Enough about my passion for poetry for a moment.

Everyone can write!

This is a genuine statement!

One of the early '*life skills*' that we humans learn is writing.

As we know, most people begin formal writing between ages three and five.

People often ask me how I wrote my books. They ask, "How do you find the time to write? Did you complete a writing degree?" Passion, opportunity, and motivation are the straightforward answers which come to mind. I begin by writing my thoughts and ideas, which soon develop into stories.

Many well-known writers do not have any formal training or degree in writing. Well, this statement is mostly true at the onset of most writing careers, but some people eventually do courses in writing and engage in formal and informal learning to become superb writers. To gain more knowledge, outstanding writers develop personalised systems and processes that help them hone their writing skills. Initially, I received no formal training in writing. However, to feel authenticated, in 2014 I completed a 6-week course in creative writing. Though it was a wonderful experience, I am not sure that it validated me, but the jury is still out on that.

You do not lose any knowledge, ever! To be a writer, you need to read and write. Do not allow the lack of formal training in writing stop you. Instead, like everything in life, learn constantly and practice writing regularly to become an excellent writer.

What is Writing?

Let us begin with the basic definition of 'writing'. Oxford Dictionary defines 'writing' as 'the art of producing something in written form so that people can read, perform, or use it'. It is also the art of putting words or letters on paper or any other surface. Anyone who can do this is a writer. Most adult human beings perform the act of writing at home, work, or elsewhere.

We are all writing. Writing is a skill which most of us already possess and often use daily.

Our writing can vary from traditional letters to text messages, emails, and social media posts.

Interestingly, many people can knit words together without copying pre-set ones off the internet. As a result, the outcomes are messages that are original, heartfelt, and inspiring. We write grocery lists, to-do lists and even felicitation messages, prayers, blessings, and commiserative messages regularly.

As a medical doctor, besides my stethoscope, my

pen is one of my vital tools. In my job as a family physician, I sign prescriptions and type up letters and patient notes. I am not alone! Many people do a lot of writing as part of their daily professional lives; however, they do not identify themselves as writers. Though, they are if we go by the above definition.

We have now established that you can write.

So, never say that you cannot write.

If you intend to be a writer, then start identifying yourself as one. Tell friends, family, neighbours, and work colleagues you are a '*writer*'. What makes you a writer is that you write. What makes you a '*good*' writer is Practice! Practice!! Practice!!!

Writing is Both a Science and an Art

I found it intriguing that one definition of writing is that it is an art or skill. However, I think it is also a science.

Let me use an analogy. Your daughter has asked you to bake and decorate a *Frozen II* cake for her 5th birthday. You can bake a perfect cake. Trust me, you can. The only caveat is that you must have the perfect recipe and use the exact quantities stated. In baking your perfect cake there is no room for flexibility. Therefore, this is the science behind baking the perfect cake, the base of your daughter's *Frozen II* cake.

The decoration of the cake is more intricate, yet more flexible.

There is room for error, especially if you are an amateur cake decorator and unlike the cake base, you can correct your mistakes several times until it is perfect. Even much better, you can invent your interpretation of the

9

Frozen II design differently, as long as your daughter can still recognise it as a *Frozen II* decorated cake. The decoration of your cake, therefore, is the art of baking.

They are both equally important. Though, I think the cake base may be slightly more so because there can be no decoration without the actual cake base. For this reason, I see the processes involved in writing the same way, as both a science and an art.

Let's look now at the foundation of your writing. This is the initial work that you do when you write all your ideas, develop your story, characters and transcribe all the thoughts in your head into a concrete form which anyone can read. Any writing that you do needs to have substance for it to be tangible. I refer to this phase as **the skeleton** of your writing. This is the science of writing, like the base of your daughter's *Frozen II cake.*

After writing all your ideas down, you need to refine and self-edit everything. Just like your cake decoration, you can tweak your work several times until you are satisfied and happy that it is fit for purpose. This is **the grind** phase of your writing.

It may require much work to improve your writing in a way that your audience understands and appreciates. This is the art in writing. Both phases are very important, but without the **skeleton** (science), there is no **grind** (art), to work on.

Why Should you Write a Book?

Writing anything, especially a book, makes us ask ourselves certain questions.

- Where do I write?

- When do I write?

- What do I write about?

- What writing style do I use?

These are all pertinent questions. However, I think the most important question to ask is, why should I write?

The answer is simple. Everyone has at least one book in them! I know this to be a statement of fact. Let us assume you write your autobiography. Your book will be unique to you, your background, experiences, and your person. Even if two people wrote on the same topic, what they write will be different in how they use words, sentences, phrases, and most likely the style. You know that I am not just making this up, this is true!

Let me take you back to the scenario of an English examination.

You are told to write an essay about a picture presented to you.

Your answers will be different unless you copy someone else's essay. The words, sentences, length, grammar, punctuation, and everything else in between will be different. You can interpret the picture and make up a story that will be unique. This is where writing differs from an exact science such as mathematics, further buttressing the fact that writing is not just science, but also an art.

"Everyone has a book in them. You have a book in you. Write it"

- Adebola Adisa

Writing is therapeutic and good for our emotional wellbeing. I do not know how many times I have resorted to writing when I felt low or had unpleasant experiences. I wrote this book "*How to Write your Book 101: Everyone has a book in them!*" during the COVID-19 pandemic. It was a challenging period, more so for health workers and their family members in terms of the risk of transmitting the Coronavirus infection. The pandemic lasted for several months and we had to make changes to our manner of working; thus, this gave me enough time to write. Nevertheless, I have also written when I have been happy. I completed most of **the skeleton** of my book "*Kaleidoscopes*" during a happy time in my life, whilst pregnant with my second daughter.

You need to write, because you have a voice, and your voice can make a difference in the world. Even if your writing touches only one life positively, it counts for a lot. Making an impact, positively or negatively, can bring about a ripple effect where we, in turn, touch other lives. They then go on to touch even more lives and the cycle goes on and on.

You also need to write because there is no room for

sitting on the wall like "Humpty Dumpty". Being indifferent can be dangerous and may cost the world lives or destinies, especially where you have the power and ability to make changes, which we all can do.

That is why news about the suicide of a celebrity CNN (Cable News Network) food journalist in 2018 inspired me to focus on writing about medical topics on social media. Many people did not understand that suicide often occurs as part of mental health disorders and did not consider the consequent helplessness of people who commit suicide. For this reason, they did not have kind things to say. It was, therefore, time to do my part in correcting wrong notions and I decided to start posting health awareness topics on my social media pages, Facebook, Twitter, and Instagram. I have never regretted this decision.

As a medical doctor, I have the experience, trained knowledge, and the voice to pass across the truth about medical conditions. The bonus is that people trust medics and believe what we say. However, not enough medical professionals are writing or trying to dispel incorrect ingrained beliefs and assumptions. Yet, there is no vacuum in nature, so people who do not understand what they are writing about or saying will keep flooding social media with lies and misconceptions and will keep misleading people, sometimes dangerously and fatally.

Another reason to write is this; even though there must be billions if not zillions of books in the world, books can never go out of fashion. I love this quote below.

"If there's a book that you want to read, but it hasn't been written yet, then you must write it."

- Toni Morrison

Writing brings our dreams, ideas, and visions to life.

Writing is powerful!

As a child, I read **Enid Blyton** books and the **Pacesetter series** later as a teenager. These books brought situations, pictures, ideas, foreign lands and otherwise unimaginable events and unreachable places alive to me there and then. They transported me into fairylands, vast possibilities, experiences and expanded my dreams.

Everything in those books felt real to me and it felt like I too was immersed in that world. I would lock myself away in rooms, spacious wardrobes, toilets, bathrooms, or other quiet spaces, just to read books, never wishing to be disturbed. I will forever cherish those precious memories. They are priceless!

Writing is creative!

As writers and through our books, we can aspire to create those alternative worlds, lives, characters, and experiences. And we can draw our readers in, giving them a chance to live their special moments.

What a privilege that is!

May I encourage you to find that book which no one has written yet. Yes, that book in you and start writing it!

Common Problems Encountered in Writing

1. What should I write about?

2. When should I write?

3. Where should I write?

4. What medium should I write on?

5. Writer's Block

   Let us look at each of these.

1. What Should I Write About?

The quick answer is that you can write on any topic and about anything. However, as a beginner, you will find that it is more realistic and safer to write on what you are passionate about. You will also find it easier. If you have a very imaginative mind or always have vivid and extraordinary dreams, chances are they are likely to be unique as it would be almost impossible for anyone else to have the exact dream as you. So why not write books on these and give your readers the chance to experience your passion.

I have always felt that authors like Stephen King write books born out of their dreams. Although, I am only guessing as I do not know this for sure.

"Write from your heart and head. Write about what makes you angry, what moves you to tears, the things about which you feel passionately. If you feel it when you write, others will feel it when they read."

- Malorie Blackman

Book genres can be grouped into two main groups: fiction and non-fiction. Many people have been able to write across different genres, so do not allow the desire to be a specific form of writer become a barrier to your writing, be flexible.

If you intend to become a '*bookpreneu*r', you may need to consider writing on topics or genres which appeal to a certain niche of readers. A *bookpreneur* is someone who makes money from book-related activities. Book titles such as 'How to Make Money off the Internet' or 'How to Get Thousands of Followers on Instagram', can draw readers in. Certain genres appeal more to book buyers, for example, romance, crime, and children's categories are well-known best-selling books.

Sometimes, our experiences and life-changing

situations allow us to become an authority in a certain genre. For instance, you might have been the first person to have accomplished a feat or passed through difficulties, survived an illness or your life suddenly changed. Or you became a first-time mum at a very young age, started a new career or innovative business venture, made millions or any other changes where you can inspire others. Such titles like "How to Become a Better Parent" or "How to Build a Business from Nothing" or "How I Survived a Stroke", may emerge.

Authors write autobiographies and biographies to tell their own stories or the achievements of famous people, politicians, survivors, high achievers, and mentors. An example is Nelson Mandela's autobiography, "*Long Walk to Freedom: The Autobiography of Nelson Mandela*". You may write to fulfil your passion for providing solutions to people's needs or because you want to inspire others.

The reason I have written this self-help book, "*How to Write your Book 101: Everyone has a book in them!*" is to guide you in writing your book. I hope you too can find the basic information and guidance which will give you the confidence to write.

If I am honest, the easiest book that I have written to date is my third book, "*#Beinspired*". "*#Beinspired*" is a compilation of poetry, quotes, medical and inspirational topics which I published as an e-book in 2019. It was a natural stress-free book for me, a bonus!

You might find the following list of the different book genres helpful.

The Different Book Genre

Fiction Books

Action/Adventure

Anthology

Classic

Comic and Graphic Novel

Crime and Detective

Drama

Fable

Fairy Tale

Fantasy

Historical Fiction

Horror

Humour

Legend

Magical Realism

Mystery

Mythology

Realistic Fiction

Romance

Satire

Science Fiction (Sci-Fi)

Short Story

Suspense/Thriller

Poetry

Non-Fiction Books

Biography

Autobiography

Essay

Memoir

Narrative Nonfiction

Periodicals

Reference Books

Self-help Book

Speech

Textbook

Poetry

Note that Poetry can be both fiction and non-fiction.

2.   When Should I Write?

Some people can write only during a specific time of the day or when no one else is in the same space as them. This may have to do with our personalities, home, or personal circumstances. In my case, I have young children, therefore, to function and have a balance in all my roles, I have had to learn to multi-task. It is the reason I have tried over the years to train myself to write whenever and wherever I can. This way, I can sit with my children in the lounge and be both a parent and a writer. Or whilst baking with them I can also write my next day's Facebook post (at least in my head), then type it up, edit and post it later. In time, you will get better at recognising what works for you and then you may wish to stick to that for better productivity. One obvious thing is that it is very important to seize every opportunity that you find to write.

The other important aspect is how often you should write. To be a serious writer, you need to write regularly, this will help you get better at crafting your words and writing.

It helps to write daily, but this is not always workable. Try to write often and, in a way, unique to you, whether it is daily or weekly.

I have written more about this further on in this book under "**How often should I write?**"

3.   Where Should I Write?

People have described having special corners, desks, quiet areas, or hideouts as their writing spaces and in fact, many well-known writers recommend this. There is absolutely nothing wrong with any of these, however, others don't need any special conditions to write. For instance, I have never needed a special room or space, but I recognise how this may be different for everyone. On the other hand, for **the grind**, the editing phase of your writing, you will need a quiet place to focus on doing a thorough job and producing an excellent book. I say write wherever it works for you. Never let spaces or the lack of spaces, or any rituals or special needs stand as an obstacle to your writing.

"I can write anywhere. I once made up the names of the characters on a sick bag while I was on an airplane." - J.K. Rowling

4. What Medium Should I Write On?

A few decades ago, we wrote in black and white; pen on paper or typed on paper using typewriters. Now we are in the digital age where it is far easier to write or type our work on computer desktops, smartphones, and other mobile devices. However, if you still wish to stay true to the old way of writing, nothing should stop you. You can also dictate using different voice-activated apps, voice recorders and audio transcription apps available on mobile devices. I always find dictation useful in situations where I suddenly have a new idea and cannot at that moment sit down to write or type.

You can consider trying that too and then transcribe your audio recordings later when it is convenient to. I use my phone for all my writing including my goals, ideas, grocery, and to-do lists. It is funny that my sister is always telling me to get a bigger phone, and she is right because I probably need one given all the writing that I do on mine.

Writing on my mobile phone is convenient because I can put down my ideas as soon as they come to mind. Other than that, it is also all-encompassing. For instance, I can research facts on the internet, check spellings or meaning of words, copy quotes and do minimal editing. I can copy, save my writing, and send it to my email. I can even switch into my social media, check posts, notifications, reply comments, and post a write-up directly, all in one breath.

Everything is just one click away! Hence, I wrote over 50% of this book on my mobile phone.

Again, it does not matter what you use, only choose what works best for you. Whatever medium you write on, and I cannot emphasise this enough, ensure that you have your work backed up, saved, or copied onto somewhere safe. Be careful to protect your original write-ups and manuscripts from damage and from being lost.

Pros and Cons of the Different Writing Media

Pen and paper

Pros

- Writing down your words on paper can connect you with your writing which can inspire more ideas and content for your book.

Cons

- It can be voluminous.

- Time- consuming.

- If you have an illegible handwriting, you or others may not be able to read it.

- You will still need to type it up or convert your write-up to digital writing.

- Can be easily lost or destroyed.

Mobile devices and Computers

Pros

- Convenient to use.

- Can be quick if you type fast.

- Can be directly edited.

- Reliable means of storage.

- Can be directly backed up and preserved.

Cons

There is room for autocorrect errors with your

words being replaced with similar-looking words.

Voice-activated/ audio transcription apps

Pros

- Easy to use.

- Quick to use.

- Hearing yourself speak can connect you with your writing and inspire more ideas and content for your book.

- Can be edited.

- Reliable means of storage.

  Cons

- The app may erroneously swap your words with similar-sounding words.

5. Writer's Block

This is a condition where a writer can't write. It can last a few hours, days and though rare, some writers experience this for several years.

Whilst some people do not believe that writer's block exists, I believe it does. It can be due to challenging circumstances, for example, your job or life gets busier, or you just had a baby or became a carer for your parents. I too have experienced periods in my life when I just could not get myself to do any piece of writing.

After I gave birth to my second daughter, it took me almost three years to get back to my book, "*Kaleidoscopes*".

Life-changing events such as loss of loved ones, divorce, sickness, or accidents can also cause writer's block. However, life-changing events can also do the exact opposite and inspire writing.

Causes of Writer's Block

There are many causes of writer's block. Let's look at some of them.

- **Physical illness**

Life happens to all of us and ongoing or new sicknesses may make it impossible or difficult for us to write. Physical illness may also lead to mental health conditions or make any pre-existing mental illness worse.

- **Mental illness**

As writing requires focus, most people will struggle to write when they are stressed at home, work or have ongoing issues in other aspects of their lives. Mental health conditions such as anxiety, depression, panic attacks, burn out and mental exhaustion may contribute to a writer's inability to write.

- **Inflexibility, for instance, confining writing to only one genre**

It is of utmost importance that we are determined from the onset, to write across different genres. There are several options to choose from, be it fiction: romance, children's writing, poetry, science fiction, legal or medical thrillers or non-fiction: autobiographies, biographies, academic writing, and guidebooks.

- **Lack of inspiration**

Whilst physical and mental illness can give rise to the lack of inspiration to write, one may not be able to point to any reason. This can happen to any writer and is well documented amongst popular writers like J.K. Rowling and Leo Tolstoy the writer of '*Anna Karenina*'. For most people, this will only be a temporary phase in their writing career.

- **Pressure and stress from having writing deadlines**

For instance, some authors have contracts to produce a certain amount of literary work over a fixed period and under specific terms and conditions. The fear of failure or pressure from this may lead to mental breakdown and inability to complete the work.

What Can You Do if You Experience Writer's Block?

1. Accept that the writer's block has happened.

Do not chew yourself up over it as that may create more stress.

2. Give yourself a goal to return to writing.

Write this goal down and stick it somewhere safe so that you won't completely forget it, for example, in a diary, on your computer files or ask someone you trust to remind you about it when they know you're ready to write again. It might be best not to stick it somewhere where you are likely to see it every day until you feel ready to, as this might add more pressure.

3. Give yourself time.

This is very important, especially if you have faced life-changing circumstances or events.

4. Be flexible.

Open your mind to writing across other genres.

5. Read plenty of books and across various topics.

Do a lot of reading.

"Read, read, read. Read; trash, classics, good or bad, and see how they do it. Just like a carpenter who works as an apprentice and studies the master. Read! You will absorb it. Then write. If it's good, you'll find out. If it's not, throw it out of the window."

-William Faulkner

6. Watch a lot of TV

Watch everything from news to movies, dramas, documentaries, and everything else of value. This will give you new ideas.

7. Join book clubs.

At book clubs, you discuss the books that you and others have read. This, in turn, will help motivate and increase your reading.

8. Brainstorm

Have discussions with others. Discuss and brainstorm on what you have read or seen or any experiences you have had.

9. Be original.

Be you! If you still feel stuck, check out what other writers are writing.

Do this only to guide you in developing your unique style and try not to copy others just to be like them. Remember that you are unique, and no two writers should be the same, otherwise what would be the point.

10. Go back to the basics

When you feel ready to try again, go back to the basics. And be deliberate about writing again.

How Often Should I Write?

Many established writers have their unique habits. For instance, some well-known authors have suggested that writers should write daily. However, I will always say, do not allow undue pressure to conform to this idea. Now let us look at the writing habits of these well-known writers.

- Stephen King writes about 6 pages of a story every day.

- Hemingway writes about 500 to 1,000 words daily.

- Haruki Murakami gets up as early at 4 am and writes for about 6 hours. Mary Angelou had similar habits.

You must remember that these are celebrity authors and no doubt got to where they did because of their dedication and hard work. You too can do the same if it works for you. However, do not forget that they are also full-time authors with no other day job. For instance, you might have a full-time 9 to 5 job and or be a parent to toddlers. Therefore, your day will be different from a retired author with no parental commitments.

Although, writing daily is a great habit to aspire to, try to do this at your own pace. Never try to be like anyone else but adapt habits to a writing style which suits you. Try to redirect the pressure you may feel into honing your writing habits and style at your own steady pace. For instance, when writing a new book, you can aim to write 100 words every day or 500 words every week.

J.K. Rowling said she writes whenever and wherever she can, during spare moments rather than at certain times or places.

I do not write every single day, some days I just cannot find the will to write. However, I desire and strive to write every day and, in this way, often end up writing on most days, but I do it all at my pace.

Can you tell the difference?

I encourage you to cultivate the habit and determination to write daily.

Do not allow the excuses of being too busy be an

obstacle to your writing either. When we are passionate about something, we always find the time to do it and may not realise how much time we have spent on it. You must find a balance to your writing in such a way that you enjoy it. Avoid getting carried away with mundane things such as your writing style, this will come to you and with experience, you will know what style best suits you.

Also, consider writing SMART writing goals for each book you decide to write.

Writing SMART Writing Goals

Do you remember **SMART** Goals? SMART is an acronym that guides you in setting your goals.

S-Specific

M-Measurable

A-Achievable

R-Realistic

T-Time Bound

Specific

Be clear and specific.

Try to answer these questions.

- What is my dream?

- Why is this important?

- What resources do I need to achieve my dream?

(e.g. illustrators, agents, time, and money)

- Who can help me?

Measurable

It is important to have measurable goals so that you can see how well you are doing, how far along you have come and how much further you need to go.

Try to answer these questions.

- How much?

- How many?

- How will I know when it is accomplished?

Achievable

Whilst it is important to have very big dreams, your goal also needs to be reachable.

Avoid setting goals that will be frustrating to achieve.

Try to answer these questions.

- How can I accomplish this goal?

- Is it possible?

For instance, it may be unrealistic to set a goal such as I will publish 1 million copies of my book in a week.

It may be more realistic to say I will publish 500 to 1000 copies of my book in 3-6 months.

Relevant

Your goal should be relevant to you and the specific issue. Remember that it is your dream, not anyone else's.

Make sure that your goal is aimed at making your dream easier to achieve.

Try to answer these questions.

- Is it necessary?

- Is it the right time?

- Is this what I want?

Time-bound

Every goal needs to have a deadline. i.e. the duration or period when it needs to get done. This will help you focus on achieving them.

Try to answer these questions.

- Is there a timeline?

- How long will it take?

- What can I do between now and a specified period?

- What can I do each day that will help me achieve my goal?

It can be very helpful to write your goals down.

When you do this, you can see the words, they almost come alive, speak to you, pull you towards them and help you reach your goals.

After writing your SMART writing goals, it usually helps to place them somewhere where you can see them daily. It can be on a vision board. I usually stick my goals of any kind on my wardrobe mirror. Here I am likely to see it every day, sometimes three or more times a day. As a result, I can read my goals to myself again and again. This has the power to steer up the mind, and the subconscious translates into physical reality such that you often achieve those goals in record time.

It has worked for me so far and many people have said the same.

So, your book's SMART writing goal could read along these lines; I will complete a 200- paged crime fiction book by June 2020 and self-edit it by September 2020. I will send it to an editor by November 2020 and self-publish it by January 2021. This is just a hypothetical goal, yours could be for a shorter or longer term.

This is how my writing goal for this book "*How to Write your Book 101: Everyone has a book in them!*" looks like.

a. Write 500 words daily.

b. Aim for 15,000 words in total.

c. Self-edit my manuscript by June 2020.

d. Professionally edit it by August 2020.

e. Market my book and encourage my target readers to preorder.

f. Publish the e-book version in September 2020.

g. Publish the paperback version in November 2020.

Do not feel frustrated if you don't achieve your book writing goals at the time you want or in the way that you want to.

Rather, learn from any delays that occur and try again.

Elements of Writing

1. What is Your Message?

Why are you writing your book?

This refers to the purpose of your book. What is the focus or message in your writing? What point do you intend to put across to your target readers? I do not think one should write without knowing why or for what purpose.

Knowing the purpose of your writing will most certainly help you narrow down your book content and assist in choosing the book title.

So, take time to find out why you are writing and determine the message or idea that you want your readers to enjoy.

2. Who are You writing for?

You need to consider the average age, gender (if applicable), profession and other specific demographic characteristics and needs of your target readers.

As you can see, identifying this will guide your language and vocabulary usage. For instance, if you are writing a medical informative book for non-medical target readers, you need to avoid medical jargon and replace them with words which they can understand without having to resort to using a medical dictionary.

Language and use of words are very important. For instance, certain words may not be acceptable or appropriate for any writing if the target is for a younger audience.

If you spend appropriate time and effort to define your target readers even before you have written your book, you will reap it all back when it is time to market your book, after it is published.

3. What is Your Writing Style?

Your writing style is how you use your words in your writing. It guides your choice of words, sentence structure and sentence length. It also gives you identity. So, in the long run, it is a magnificent way to stand out from other writers in your genre.

There are distinct writing styles; expository, descriptive, persuasive, and narrative. Some people recognise a fifth writing style; creative writing. Creative writing is an art of making things up and the primary aim is to entertain the target readers.

Many writing styles already encompass the creative writing style.

a. Expository writing explains processes and focuses on facts. We often see this style in textbooks, recipes, news articles and scientific writing. The writing style in this book "*How to Write your Book 101: Everyone has a book in them!*" is expository.

b. Descriptive writing is exactly what it says on the label.
It is used when describing, for instance, a person or

character or event, etc.

We often see this style used in poetry, journal writing and blogs. I wrote an enormous part of my third book, "*#Beinspired*" in this style.

c. Persuasive writing seeks to convince the readers about something or someone and is often the opinion of the writer only and not necessarily factual. Editorials, reviews, and advertisements are often written in this way.

d. Narrative writing tells a story or many stories.

Novels, short stories, autobiographies, biographies, and poetry are often written in this style. It allows the readers to become immersed in the story and connect with it. I love to write in the narrative and believe that it is my natural writing style because it is the one, I find most effortless.

I wrote my books "*The Magic of Destiny*" and "*Kaleidoscopes*" in the narrative style. In these books, the readers can often feel as if they are living the story themselves. And this is the feedback most of my readers have given me, so job done!

Time and experience should be your companions in

helping you develop a specific writing style or a variety of writing styles.

4. Grammar, spelling, punctuation, word usage, sentences, paragraphs, layout, typographical errors, and organisation

These are essential for any book to appear professionally written. The way to simplify this is to write in a language which you already understand how to speak and write. Self-editing your draft will also be easier if you write in a familiar language.

Apart from the English language, I also speak my native language, Yoruba, which I also can write, but not too well. It is far easier for me to write in the English language which I was taught to read and write in. I have spoken it all my life and feel comfortable conversing in it. This does not stop me from dreaming of translating my books into the Yoruba language, however, I know that I can't do this without professional help.

There are various free and cost-effective software packages which can help you polish your writing and correct all the elements listed above, including spelling, grammar, and punctuation. I have written more about this further on in this book under "**the grind**".

How Do You Find the Inspiration for Your Writing?

I will let you in on a secret about my third book "*#Beinspired*". Unlike my first two books, "*The Magic of Destiny*" and "*Kaleidoscopes*", I did not sit down to write "*#Beinspired*". In the two years before the time I published "*#Beinspired*", I had written several posts for my social media pages, regularly posting about two or three articles every week. These articles comprised medical issues, poetry, quotes, and any personal experiences which I felt could inspire, encourage, and motivate my readers. Over time, my posts gathered momentum, comments, and wonderful reactions, especially on Facebook. As a result, I was constantly receiving messages and calls about how I was impacting people's lives positively.

So, it felt right to put together a compilation of my most impactful articles over the said period. I formatted and published them as an e-book on the ***Okadabooks*** publishing platform.

As you can see, we can write our books to fulfil people's needs or to solve problems or questions being asked. Any book written in this way will always be a purposeful one. Frequent requests, therefore, from friends and readers asking me about how they can write their books, inspired me to write this book, "*How to Write your Book 101: Everyone has a book in them!*".

Even if you have been uncertain about how to begin your writing journey, this book is your answer. It will equip you to write your book too!

How to Improve Your Writing

1. Read! Read!! Read!!!

Read wide and be flexible. When you read a lot, across a variety of genres and a variety of materials, you will gain a vast amount of knowledge. Consequently, you will also build up a vast vocabulary and this will come in handy when you write your book. It is that simple.

"If you don't have time to read, you don't have the time (or the tools) to write. Simple as that."

Stephen King

2. View! View!! View!!!

Watch a variety of movies, drama, YouTube videos and other images across a variety of genres

Images help to create vivid ideas. If you can see it,

you can be it.

3. Write regularly, if possible, daily

I have already discussed this earlier in the book.

4. Focus on your writing and on writing as a profession

I am not suggesting that you quit your day job, but if you intend to have people take you seriously as a writer, dedicate time to your writing. This helps to nurture your writing skills and allows it to grow.

5. Don't give up on your drafts

Even if they do not appear to amount to much, keep them all and go back to refine them again and again.

6. Dream big, but start small, everyone must start from somewhere

The reality is that majority of writers will never become popular authors or become wealthy from writing, however, everyone can achieve their dream of writing their book.

Be determined to work hard, persevere, and make good use of every opportunity which comes your way.

7. Be original and avoid trying to be like someone else

You are different; your background and experiences are also unique. So, if you dig deep enough, you will always come up with something special.

The Phases of Writing

I have described the processes involved in writing in three phases:

- the conception

- the skeleton and

- the grind

Think of these processes as more of a cycle rather than a one-directional three-phase process.

See the cycle diagram below.

THE PHASES OF WRITING CYCLE DIAGRAM

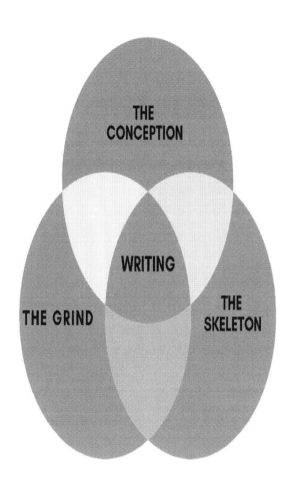

A. The Conception

We conceive dreams, visions, and desires in our mind. Our brains are exceptional, very rich and have a lot of potential. Whereas, if you cannot dream, it will be difficult to achieve many things. Dreams are magnificent, and everyone should have big dreams

Thus, **the conception** is a very vital phase in our writing journey, and it is almost impossible to write anything without ever thinking about it.

Just like dreams, our writing or books often form in our minds as daydreams, night dreams and visions.

We can nurture **the conception** phase by making deliberate efforts to learn from the work of others, reading and watching materials across a variety of genres. Remember that **the conception** is not a one-off process and even during the editing phases of our drafts, we must keep coming back to form more ideas, develop our characters and storylines. It is like coming back to the drawing board, so to say.

B. The Skeleton

Dreams are only beneficial to you because no one else has access to them until you tell them. If you are bold enough to tell people about your dreams, the next step is to write them down. We all know how easy it is to forget our dreams and ideas if we do not immediately write them down. Do not just leave your ideas in your head, if you do not develop and act on them, they just remain dreams. I sound like a broken record saying this again, but I cannot overemphasise this. If you forget to write them down, can you imagine how much the world would lose out from not being able to benefit from your unique ideas? Writing things down also inspires you, it is the evidence that what you have is real and not just a pipe dream.

Thus, those messy initial drafts on paper or notes which you have kept on your mobile devices or computers are what I like to call **the skeleton**. The **skeleton** may also refer to the characters in your book. Once you create the characters say in your fiction story, you can then add on the *muscles, tendons, and the skin* by slowly developing that character.

I always advise people to just write whatever they have, anything at all to start with. Even if your drafts appear to be rubbish, try not to be hard on yourself. Never mind that they appear strange or that no one can make sense or head or tail of what you have written, or that at times even you cannot!

Make no mistake, your draft is gold. Never dismiss them or lose them. Never!

The editing will come later, and you can always refine whatever you have written.

"Start writing, no matter what. The water does not flow until the faucet is turned on."

-Louis L'Amour

So, put those dreams down on a hard device, on something concrete and safe. Put them on a **medium**.

Whatever medium you use, make sure you back up your work just in case something weird happens to your hard drive, device, or paper manuscript. For example, a fire outbreak might damage it, or it may accidentally drop in the water or your device can just crash. Pardon me, but when it comes to my draft, I usually assume the worst scenarios. I feel the need to belabour this point because you would have invested a lot of passion and time into your work. I once lost some drafts meant for my social media posts, never to be retrieved. Even though I eventually rewrote the articles, it never had the same nice ring to it. So, I know the pain and regret that this brings. Therefore, my shortcut method is to email my drafts to my secure email and update this each time I do any further editing.

One other important reason to back up your work is that we now live in a world where some unscrupulous characters develop viruses every day and some of these can remotely access and attack everything that you have saved on your computer.

Hence, do not forget to have adequate antivirus protection for your computer and any other media that you write on.

To sum it up, the **skeleton** is the foundation of your book. I believe that it is the most important phase needed in your writing process.

C. The Grind

The grind is otherwise known as the self-editing phase. It is what you do to your skeleton and is one of the more challenging phases of writing. Self-editing your draft and achieving a good flow to your writing requires dedication, patience, tenacity, and hard work. Depending on the type of writing, some of us will only need to dedicate several hours to **the grind,** whereas others will require many days, even months. You may become frustrated and feel like stopping. Know that it might be okay to pause for a while until you feel able to continue. Nevertheless, you must strive to keep your determination to complete your work someday. Never quit, you must keep going!

There are several ways to simplify this phase using available resources, some of which are free and others affordable. These include software like grammar and spelling checkers. Most computer systems already have spelling, punctuation mark and grammar tools, such as editor on **Microsoft Word**, but you can take this a notch higher by using other online editing software such as **Grammarly**, **ProWritingAid** and **AutoCrit**. **Grammarly** highlights commonly misused words, spelling, and grammatical errors. **ProWritingAid** does a similar check but also highlights overused, repetitive words and sentences. Some software packages have basic free to use resources and offer affordable premium options. I have used both **Grammarly** and **ProWritingAid** and found **Grammarly** more user friendly. Please be aware that when you use online software, there is a slight risk of having your manuscript stolen. However, the risk is minimal, unless you are already a well-known author.

Formatting is a major key to your book appearing well-polished and professional. This includes the font style, font size, spacing and paragraphing. Depending on the book genre, editors often recommend using Times New Roman font style, in size 12, left alignment and double-spaced line spacing which makes your text easier to read. Also, consider your paragraph spacing and indentation. These are all available to amend on the Microsoft word document.

It may be important to cite your text, depending on your writing genre. For instance, in academic or factual writing and when writing biographies and autobiographies.

Be consistent with your referencing style: APA, MLA, Chicago, Harvard etc.

If you are writing in the English language, be consistent with one form of spelling, using either the United States or United Kingdom versions. This is important because many words are written differently. For instance, color versus colour, center versus centre, recognize versus recognise, respectively. Also, be aware of vocabulary differences. For instance, vacation versus holiday, elevator versus lift and sweater versus jumper, for American and British English vocabularies, respectively.

All the above points are also important if you are getting your book edited by an editor or for academic writing or essays. Some editors have strict requirements which you need to follow when submitting your work to them. Again, you are not obliged to conform to a fixed format style, but I am sure you can see the benefit in doing what many editors recommend.

You are likely to find that formatting is easier to get on with if you have written your draft and saved it on non-traditional media such as mobile devices and computers rather than on pen and paper. However, even if you have done your writing on paper or dictated on audio recorders, don't be discouraged. Now that you need to get your work typed, you can do it yourself or pay someone to do it. However, if you pay someone, ensure that you get this done at a stipend especially if you intend to publish and sell your books. Remember that all the costs add up to increase the price of each unit book. On the other hand, if you intend to self-edit your book with no professional help, then you must get very close to perfection during this phase. Avoid cutting corners because you will soon find that you still need to come back and revisit any issues which you delay or completely ignore.

When you have completed your self-editing, read your finished product, and leave it to rest for some time, then read it again. Next, read it aloud to yourself, thinking of it as a book written by someone else and which you paid for. You may also consider asking your trusted friends or colleagues to have a look and tell you what they think.

I encourage you not to give up during **the grind** phase, no matter how long it takes, keep going until you have achieved your dreams whether it is an article or a published book. I am not sure if there is anything such as a perfect book. Though, you can attain writing a very good or near-perfect book, so yes, do your best, but do not overdo the editing.

"Trying is not failure, however, the lack of trying may well be".

-Adebola Adisa

My Top Tips for Writing

1. Why are You Writing?

Write not just for the sake of writing, money, or fame. Write to make a positive difference in people's lives. The money may even come later, but may I suggest that it should not be your focus, but a bonus!

Also, be specific about who you are writing for, you cannot write for everyone.

2. Decide on Your Genre

In my fiction book "*Kaleidoscopes*", I focused on women's health, specifically HIV/AIDS and lifestyle issues. However, as previously discussed under **The Different Book Genre**, books can be broadly grouped into fiction or non-fiction and there are a thousand and one genres that you can write on. You could decide to write biographies or be a social critic. It is easier to maintain your tempo of writing if you write on what you know, what you are good at and what you are passionate about.

3. Choose Your Favourite Medium

My favourite medium is my mobile phone. On the other hand, yours may be a pen on paper. You may even record on audio devices and get it typed up later.

4. Challenge Yourself and Choose the D- Day for Starting

You can start jotting down your plans, ideas, thoughts, dreams and slowly develop it. Keep doing so and work hard. Set your writing goals and challenge yourself. Consider writing regularly; daily, weekly, or even monthly if that is all you can manage for the time being. Whilst I believe that writing should be flexible in terms of when you should write and where you should write on, you still need to define your writing goals.

Do not forget to write your SMART writing goals.

5. Back up your Work

I remember when I was editing my book "*Kaleidoscopes*", I was afraid that a virus would wipe off several years' worth of writing, so I always forwarded an updated copy of my book to my email address each time I worked on it. You can save your work on your desktop hard drive, SD cards or other forms of removable storage devices. Most computers autosave when you edit documents, however, it is important to check that this function works or better still, save your work at intervals whilst working, for instance, you may manually save every few minutes. You can also make photocopies of paper notes and keep them in a safe place. When I write shorter notes, I find it convenient to send them as text messages to myself.

Other avenues to secure your work include software such as Back up, Dropbox, Google Drive, Microsoft OneDrive, and many Cloud Backup solutions, some of which may be free or cheap.

6. Learn! Learn!! Learn!!!

Read books, articles, newspapers, magazines, and everything available across a variety of genres. Watch 'how-to' YouTube videos too. I have found that these can improve and add value to your writing.

Make it a habit to learn about how to improve your writing. Attend online or face-to-face training courses in writing, you will find many free online resources and if you can afford to, pay for them.

7. Join a Book Club

Be part of a community who discuss and or critique books. You will learn a lot. It is also important to keep improving yourself and reviewing your work and the work of others, ensuring that you learn from them.

Moreover, if you engage well enough, your book club may read and critique your book for you. Nevertheless, if you do this, ensure that your work will be safe and be ready to face any criticism with grace.

8. Have a Book Mentor

A book mentor is an experienced writer who will guide you through your book writing journey, helping you to identify and avoid common pitfalls. They can also double-up as someone to whom you are accountable, who will check up on your writing. Being accountable to someone often helps you to become steadfast and consistent.

9. Also, have a Writing Partner or Buddy

A book partner or buddy is someone who may also be writing their book, and they may or may not be at your writing pace. Find someone willing to brainstorm and share ideas about your writing. This relationship will probably keep you going when you want to quit. Make sure your book buddy differs from your book mentor.

10. Celebrate your Victories

Even if they are small, remember to pat yourself on the back for every completed stage or phase of your book. For instance, when you complete a chapter or the development of a new character or storyline. Not only will this boost your confidence, but it will also carry you through to the next completed phase and guess what, you get to celebrate that too.

11. Do Not Give Up

Have a determination to complete whatever writing you start, even if it takes years. If you ever abandoned any writing in the past, I know how you feel because I have been there too. I abandoned my book "*Kaleidoscopes*" for about three years during which I became a mum of two, completed my training as a family doctor and got on with other aspects of my life. Did I ever feel guilty or unaccomplished? No! I knew that my manuscript was somewhere safe and when the time felt right, I would continue from where I had stopped. And sure, enough I did and finished writing it.

"Time makes things clearer and brighter! The benefit of time is like the experience one has after squinting for so long, and upon wearing the perfect prescription lenses, suddenly everything comes into focus."

-Adebola Adisa

12. Write! Write!! Write!!!

I cannot reiterate this enough. There isn't any shortcut. If you have the best ideas, but you are not doing any writing at all, you are not a writer. You are a writer because you write, it is as simple as that!

Ethical and Legal Aspects of your Writing

A. Avoid Plagiarism

Plagiarism is passing off someone else's writing as yours. It is a crime in some countries and even if this is not so in yours; it is morally wrong. Do not forget that there are detection, text matching and anti-plagiarism software which can assist in the detection of plagiarism.

B. Legal Aspects

Consider the legal implications of your book content and ensure that you write based on facts, especially, when writing biographies, autobiographies, research topics, or in academic writing. In this instance, you can use references as proof.

Editing

Once satisfied with all the processes involved in writing, i.e., the **conception**, the **skeleton** and the **grind**, the next stage is to **edit**.

You would have done a lot of self-editing before arriving at this stage. Therefore, **editing** here refers to the checks by others, in most cases professional editors. It is important to avoid cutting corners during editing because this will only result in poorly edited books which may ruin your reputation and future as an author.

Avoid rushing your book editing timeline. I remember setting a target to publish and launch my book, "*Kaleidoscopes*" by my 40th birthday.

Even though I had about three months to spare from the deadline, I have never felt so pressured in my life and almost had to cancel the book launch. I don't think I will ever do that to myself again.

You can have your book edited as many times as you wish to and until you are satisfied. Recently, I looked through several pages of my poetry collection and discovered that some of them seemed childish, much like rhymes, so I plan to re-edit them. You can change your work to suit whatever purpose you wish it to; it is all yours.

For instance, I can refine the tone in my poetry so they will suit an older audience. I have amended my poem 'Life's Good' many times and now am satisfied with the finished work. You will find 'Life's Good' at the end of this book.

"You have to write the book that wants to be written. And if the book will be too difficult for grown-ups, then you write it for children."

-Madeleine L'Engle

If you intend to publish your book, it is best to get it edited by an editor. This will cost you money, but there are cost-effective options available. Think about starting to save up for your book editing, the moment you write. Though rare, it is possible to get it done free if the editor is a family member, friend, or mentor. You may also get free editing as part of a book publishing package.

Try to negotiate a good deal, for instance, face to face or drop-in sessions or as many editing cycles as might be necessary. On the other hand, if you are going down the non-professional editing route, (which I will not advise) then it is wise to ask two or three people to read through your write-up or manuscript at different times. Ensure that they are trustworthy, and this is also true when using a professional editor. Check their terms and conditions and formatting requirements for the submission of your work. Editing may take a few weeks or months, or even longer, depending on the length of your manuscript and the editor, so ensure that you have agreed on deadlines too.

After the initial editing, review your work. If you make further changes, send the amended work back to the editor to look through again until you are both satisfied. Remember that unless the corrections are grammatical, structural, or spelling mistakes, you do not have to accept all the comments and suggestions. This is your work, which I suggest that you guard jealously because you are the one with the ideas and vision and are the only person who knows exactly how your book should look like. However, if you have paid to have your work edited and your editor is reliable and experienced, then it might be in your best interest to accept most, if not all the suggestions.

Other Important Aspects of Your book

The Book Title

Ask yourself the following questions

- What is the purpose of my book? i.e. why am I writing this book?

- Who are my target readers? i.e. who am I writing for?

- What type of book is it? i.e. what is my writing style?

If you already answered these questions at the start of your writing (**Elements of Writing**), you would find it easier to decide on your book title.

Try to fit your title to the vision that you have for your book. Your book title needs to be catchy enough to engage potential readers, encourage them to linger enough for them to not only consider reading your book but also part with their money to buy it. Do not sell a title which does not depict the contents of your book. That would be dishonest!

It is also important to use a title which is not time-limited. For instance, I wrote this book during the COVID-19/ new coronavirus pandemic and thought that a title like ' *How to Write Your Book During this COVID-19 Pandemic*' would be very catchy. However, I kept asking myself one vital question; would it be timeless? The answer was always, no.

The Pandemic has been a devastating period which we will all remember for a long time. But for how long? Until the next generation, maybe! My vision for this book is to provide the key learning points for aspiring and unknown writers. I also want to help them build the confidence to write and establish themselves as writers who can inspire other unknown writers. My awareness that this dream transcends several generations helped me decide on my book title.

The Body of Your Work

The first few words in your book are very important. They have the power to invite and draw in your reader but can also put them off reading your book. The body of your work needs to hold on to the captured attention of your target readers.

Consider the following

1. Start with strong and captivating punchlines.

2. Use tactics such as creating initial shock or surprise, asking questions, describing a character, or setting.

3. Strive to write authentic content. Being genuine brings a deeper connection to your readers.

4. Avoid overgeneralisation, instead, be specific and descriptive.

5. Write simply, clearly, and concisely. Avoid complicated, vague words and jargon.

6. Avoid using unnecessary and overused words such as more, very, and really.

7. Avoid repetitive words, sentences, and scenarios.

8. Try not to use clichés, unless it brings more meaning to what you are describing.

9. Where possible, replace three to four words with one simpler word e.g. 'in order to' can be replaced with 'to'.

10. Consider replacing adverbs with more impactful words such as adjectives. e.g. you can replace 'gently' with 'docile' or 'sweetly' with 'charming'.

"Omit needless words."

-William Skunk

The Garnishes

I refer to those aspects which beautify any book as the **garnishes**. These include the chapter guide, appreciation, dedication, and author's biography. Certain book illustrations may come under here too. Remember that illustrations are a major part of many categories of children's book writing, especially the younger age group and in this case cannot be considered as garnishes. Depending on the writer you are, you might find many of these **garnishes** unnecessary if they do not add or take away anything from your book content. In fact, I have read some e-books which have done away with them. Some readers skip these too.

I think I learnt it the hard way. When I republished "*The Magic of Destiny*" under my pen name Jessica Dice, I omitted the author biography and picture since the whole point was to use a pseudo-name to widen my target readers. However, I regretted that decision. Thankfully, I had a second chance with "*Kaleidoscopes*" and went to town, adding in all the extras, including a full-page black-and-white picture of myself.

I love the **garnishes** and find them essential. For me, they are the part of your book where you do not have to stick to any rules in book writing. Your readers can learn about you; thus, you can satisfy their curiosity in the author's biography page. It is where I can express myself and share my favourite quotes or interests with my readers. The appreciation and dedication pages allow you to express gratitude to people who have helped make your book a reality.

However, there are no hard and fast rules, and you can decide what you wish to include or exclude.

Synopsis

Have you ever read a headline or the back-page summary of a book that is so enticing you want to pick it up, borrow or buy it there and then! The experience is meant to feel like you have been punched in the face and would not recover until you have read that book.

The synopsis is a concise description or summary of your book. You need to dedicate effort and time to come up with a convincing punchline that can convert your readers from being window shoppers, into paying or committed readers. This is a challenging feat, considering that you will need to summarise your entire book page count into a few brief lines. However, it is entirely possible if you prioritise and practise writing it.

A synopsis could also be your pitch to literary agents if you seek to publish your book through the traditional publishing route. Writing a good synopsis is an aspect of copyrighting and you will find useful copyrighting resources online.

Book Cover

You already know that your synopsis could be the deal-breaker for your target readers. The graphic design on your front cover and your photograph too can either attract or dissuade them from buying your book. I suggest a careful reflection on your book cover before making any firm decision. Consider having your cover photograph taken by a professional photographer.

Most publishing houses have a vast collection of graphic designs and colours to choose from. Although, if you already have an idea, it is best to explain this to the graphic designer through your book publishing consultant. You may wish to ask trusted family and friends to assist with your choice at this stage. That is entirely up to you, but make sure you are 100% satisfied before submitting and signing off your choice.

Think About Answering These Questions Before Publishing Your Book

1. Why should anyone read your book?

2. What benefit will your book bring to your readers; value for money, entertainment, education, awareness, facts of life, health or spiritual?

3. Are your synopsis and book title suitable fits for your content?

4. If it is a memoir, have you written facts, did you avoid lies, ethical and legal dilemmas, and any possibility of lawsuits?

5. If your book is making a promise to fulfil needs in your target readers, have you achieved this?

Publishing

If you are anything like me, publishing your book is probably what is utmost on your mind when you write, and you want to get it done as soon as possible. It is possible to write and publish your work within a brief period through motivation, dedication, hard work and focused time. Decide on what form you want to publish your manuscript. You can publish e-books, paperbacks or audiobooks or a combination of all three. Also think about the type of publishing method you intend to use; independent, traditional, or self-publishing.

Independent publishing also known as Indie publishing is a newer form of publishing where you do everything yourself; write, publish, edit, do the cover graphic designs and market your books. Some people also publish their books. Many still consider Indie publishing as part of self -publishing.

On the other hand, the traditional publishing route is highly competitive but not impossible to find. If you would rather publish your book under traditional publishing houses, save time by finding out what genre they are looking for. For instance, traditional publishers are usually interested in children's books. Do your research, then write and submit your manuscript to several publishers and do not quit until you secure your book contract. You can also find literary agents to do the leg work and connect you with book publishers. Like anything in life, if we keep trying without giving up, we will find the way.

If you wish to self -publish, there are several choices. Find book publishing offers, sales or promotions to reduce the cost of each unit book. Also, ensure that you understand the important details, what it includes or excludes, the terms and conditions of the package you intend to buy. For instance, do you have limitless correction cycles or a limited number after which you incur charges?

Seven years ago, I bought a two for one book publishing package through which I published my books "*The Magic of Destiny*" in 2014 and "*Kaleidoscopes*" in 2018. Notice that I was able to publish them 4 years apart because the deal did not have an expiry date, whereas others may do. That same package included e-book and paperback publishing, ISBN for each book version, 10 free illustrations, a free website and hosting for a year, a free content check to ensure that the language was suitable for younger target readers, marketing via Amazon and Author house websites and two paperback copies of each book. It did not include any professional editing of my books.

The publishing process is often simple and quick if there are no issues with the content and language, or other errors. Everything could be concluded in only a few weeks. Your publisher will usually assign a publishing consultant to you and will provide you with various online forms which allow you to write your preferences; formatting, page layout, graphic design for your book cover, synopsis, illustrations, photographs and other ideas that you may have.

Simple Steps Involved in Self –Publishing

1. Purchase your book publishing package.

A book publishing consultant or someone with a similar role will be assigned to you.

2. You may need to register an author account with the publisher.

3. Your book publishing consultant will go over the details of all the steps involved.

4. Submit your manuscript through an approved email address or other agreed format.

5. Confirm that your publisher has received your manuscript.

6. Confirm that your manuscript has passed a content check.

7. Choose your book cover, submit your synopsis and garnishes if any.

8. You will receive the electronic proofs of your manuscript.

9. Take time to review your electronic proofs and make the necessary corrections

10. Once satisfied, sign off your book content or galley, and book cover designs.

11. Agree and sign off the book pricing schedule.

12. Other processes include the Quality Assurance checks, evaluation for copyright and legal issues.

Once your book passes all these checks and evaluation, it is sent off for the final stage which is the printing.

Note that these are only the basic steps and yours may differ depending on the type of book, your publisher, and the publishing package that you have purchased.

Once approved, your publisher usually sends a copy of your book to you. This is your proof copy which allows you to see what your book looks and feels like. I remember the exhilarating feeling I experienced when I received my first published book. I get the exact feeling with each new book I write and publish. You too will have this feeling when you publish your book and I promise that it is one worth waiting for!

However, it is not over yet, you now need to check the proof copy. You must read through it from front-to-back cover. You will have to check that all your ideas have been well interpreted.

Is this what you wanted?

Painstakingly check for errors. If possible, ask a trusted person to read it too. The publishers still allow you to make corrections at this stage.

Once satisfied, inform your publisher, and it is then that they will complete your publishing process. At last, it is done. Congratulations!

Marketing

Now that you have done all the hard work and published your book, you just want to celebrate and relax. However, it is not the time to rest on your oars just yet, you need to inform your readers and market your book to them. If you self-published your book, you would need to work very hard to market it, unless it becomes a bestseller overnight or you are already a well-known author or celebrity.

Do not doubt yourself or think that no one will buy your book. Start by selling to your family and friends, they will buy your books, but if they decide not to, just sanction them! Okay, disclaimer, do not take this seriously.

I have found out that if you are just starting as an author; you need to connect with people one on one. I have sold more books in this way and through smaller meetings than through large gatherings. If people know you and feel your passion in your books, they are more likely to buy them.

With over 7 billion people in the world, thinking that no one will read what you put out, is a blatant lie. Some readers are looking to buy and read the exact book or story that you have written; you only need to strategise how to reach them. The most important marketing strategy in today's world is social media marketing. This is a very systematic process which you must find out more about and master.

So then, let's look further at things to consider for marketing.

1. When marketing your book on social media, always think about your target readers. Ask yourself these questions.

- Who are my target readers?

- What do my target readers do?

- Where do my target readers find their books?

- What kind of content are my target readers looking for?

- Can I identify which book titles or content are similar to mine?

2. You can save time by starting your book marketing even before publishing it.

3. Plan how to market your book on the different social media platforms, Amazon, Facebook, Instagram, LinkedIn etc.

4. Have a book launch or book reading and signing event.

5. Think about the unit cost of your book. The lower the cost, the more accessible it is likely to be.

5. Slowly build your niche of loyal readers and fans.

7. Think about book sales and promo.

8. Get reviews for your book.

9. Consider having a website where you can direct your target readers and as an avenue to collect their email addresses.

10. Consider starting a blog or featuring as a guest writer in other people's social media platforms.

Summary of My Tips for Writing

Let us sum up on how you can write your book.

1. Define the purpose of your writing.

2. Decide on your genre

3. Choose your medium.

4. Decide when you will start writing (write your SMART writing goals)

5. Save and backup your work.

6. Learn! Learn!! Learn!!!

7. Join a book club.

8. Find a book mentor.

9. Have a writing buddy.

10. Celebrate completed stages of your book writing.

11. Complete whatever you start writing.

12. Write! Write!! Writc!!!

Conclusion

Thank you for reading my book, "*How to Write your Book 101: Everyone has a book in them!*". You have now equipped yourself with the basic and effective tools that will guide you on how to write your book. The main take-home message in this book is that there is a book in you, so stop delaying and start writing now! Remember to keep my top tips for writing at your fingertips.

It would be nice to hear from you, so please share your thoughts about how this book has helped you. Share it with your friends and family too. Also, write to tell me about any experiences in your writing journey. You can email ***dradebolaadisa78@gmail.com*** or contact me via my website dradebolaadisa.com.

Do not forget that I can also assist with the initial self-editing of your books and offer cost-effective one to one author support services.

I will conclude by sharing a piece of my heart with you; one of my favourite poems.

Life's Good

Life's good

Live it to the fullest

Perceive it

It gives so much hope

Love each day

Touch it

Enjoy every moment

Own it

Help someone to live it

Never limit it

Don't restrict it

Life is a gift

Cherish it

Live it to the fullest

Remember that you don't own it

You can't create it

Protect it

You got it free

Breathe it

Recharge it

Walk it with someone

That special someone

Teach them to love it

Don't snuff it out

Stop!

Don't pollute it

Value it

Live it to the fullest

Train in it

Bless each day that you see it

Feel it

Do not abandon it

Experience it

Be it

Birth it

Never kill it

Grow it

Nurture it

Feed it until it blossoms

Clothe it

It is yours to adore

Be thankful for it

Shelter it

Life is everyone you meet

Celebrate it

Life is good

Live it to the fullest

Adebola Adisa

2007

❤❤❤

Testimonials

"I had the privilege of meeting Dr Adebola Adisa on a friend's Facebook page. She offered to go through my writing with me.

Being a first-timer, she was patient with me and encouraged me to develop my characters. She also pointed out that the book should have a purpose that I would like it to fulfil. She tagged me to her write-ups, and they have been very enlightening.

Her words gave me a focus and made me more organized in my writing. I appreciate that she did this from her busy schedule and for free too!"

-Barr. Yetunde Ebele Alabi

Aspiring Author

"Dr Adebola Adisa is a prolific and intelligent writer exuding her extravagant depth of practical wisdom. Her words are like choice silver, bringing understanding to the simple. Beyond this, she has been a great support and backbone to other writers especially me - She's one who supported morally, intellectually, and financially in my adventure in publishing my first book - QUEST. Indeed, she is a woman of LIGHT and you just want to read from or be around someone who can help you turn the LIGHTS ON. My place in her heart is booked. Book yours!"

-Paul-Adekunle Adèbowale Jr

Author 'The Quest'

"I reached out to Adebola as I was trying to self-publish. I realised she had done a few books from a group we are both on. She was quick to respond to my queries and offered massive support, especially after I published my book. Though we haven't met, she's been very courteous towards me and always lovely. It's been a pleasure knowing her."

-Dr Abimbola Morakinyo

Author 'Big Hair Day'

"I reached out to Dr Adebola Adisa when I was wondering how to make my books available to the public. She shared with me her experience of publishing her books. She was ever so supportive, suggesting the different options available and supplying me with links to contact publishers. It was a relief to speak to someone who had a first-hand experience. It made the job easier than I expected."

-Dr Omobola Jeffreys

Founder Thy Precious Jewel

Author 'Mum's Altar and Possessing the Gate'

"I have had the support of Dr Adebola Adisa with the writing of my book: The Naija Food Philosopher. It is an unusual book as it is themed around Nigerian Food.

I have been wary of giving the manuscript to people to read and I was afraid that some people might not 'get it'.

I, however, found Dr Adebola to be approachable. She allayed any apprehension I might have had.

I have read her posts on Facebook in which she

encourages writers to put their thoughts on paper. She is an author, and I have read with interest the various articles and books she had written.

I needed someone to read through my manuscript and first and foremost, tell me if it was readable and screen for errors.

As a General Practitioner, I knew she would be busy, and I was pleasantly surprised when she told me she had just boarded a train for London and was reading the manuscript during her journey.

She read through and gave me encouraging feedback. She also suggested the restructuring of parts of the manuscript which I took on board.

She devotes time to reading, and I find that inspiring. I know she is involved in her charity; Brave Hearts and I am amazed at her being able to juggle the various demands on her time with ease.

I highly recommend her as a support for any writer needing help along their literary journey."

-Dr Wilson Orhiunu

GP & Author 'My Time and Love Letters'

"Adebola is a known author and accomplished writer.

Asides publishing her books, she writes regularly about pertinent health and social issues on social media reaching a diverse audience. She spurred me on while I was writing my book and assisted in editing it. She also signposted me on my journey to self-publishing."

-Dr Adebola Hassan

Medical Doctor and Author

My Published Books

THE MAGIC OF DESTINY

What does not kill you makes you stronger! Kike is bold and determined. In "*The Magic of Destiny*", she takes us down memory lane; her childhood, adulthood, family life, friendships, faith, and all that her life entails. Even though she did not know it, her life was about to be marred by a deep and personal tragedy.

Will she sink in the rough seas of despair and violation, or ride the waves, and emerge a survivor?

Writing "*The Magic of Destiny*"

"*The Magic of Destiny*" is my first book. I wrote it when I was still trying to find my feet in my medical career. It was a challenging period for me; I was feeling unsatisfied with the uncertainties and lack of opportunities facing my medical career. Writing the skeleton of "*The Magic of Destiny*" was very speedy. If I recollect correctly, I completed my manuscript within a few short weeks. Then a chance meeting with Dr Steve Shaba, publisher and founder of Kraft Books, Nigeria made me realise that I could publish my book. So, I rushed through self-editing my manuscript and published "*The Magic of Destiny*" under Kraft Books, Nigeria, in 2008.

In 2014, I bought a 2 for 1 self-publishing package with Author House and went on to re-edit and republish "*The Magic of Destiny*", this time under a pseudo-name to get a wider and unrestricted audience.

I am frequently asked if "*The Magic of Destiny*" is my real-life story. The answer is no; it isn't. Although it is entirely fictional, I can recognise myself, family, and friends in Kike's story.

"*The Magic of Destiny*" is available on Amazon, okadabooks.com and from my website dradebolaadisa.com. See links below.

https://okadabooks.com/book/about/the_magic_of_destiny/28004#.XRyu99bQ9PI.

https://www.amazon.co.uk/Magic-Destiny-Second-Jessica-Dice-ebook/dp/B0792LH8QY/ref=mp_s_a_1_3?keywords=jessica+dice&qid=1579072993&sr=8-3

KALEIDOSCOPES

There is no better way to tell your story than when you tell it yourself.

Yet, no one wants to hear your story when it is about the dreaded HIV and AIDS. These women refuse to give in to fear and tell their story, they must.

10 women!

10 stories!!

1 virus!!!

Writing "*Kaleidoscopes*"

I began writing "*Kaleidoscopes*" in late 2015, but life happened, I got swamped and abandoned my writing. In early 2018, I found a new drive and began writing again. I self-published later that year and launched "*Kaleidoscopes*" on my 40th birthday.

My experience as a young doctor; challenges, fears, uncertainties, and the confidence which I later developed inspired "*Kaleidoscopes*". As a young house-officer, I remember how scared I was when I accidentally got a needlestick injury; I feared that I could be HIV positive. Though, I found out later that all was well, at that moment I could feel and imagine the state which anyone living with HIV could be in, except that they had to live that way every day of their lives. Their fear is one which is clouded by unacceptable stigmatization, fuelled by the lack of knowledge and unawareness about HIV/AIDS. So, I wrote "*Kaleidoscopes*" to promote public awareness and educate my readers about HIV/AIDS.

"*Kaleidoscopes*" is available on Amazon, okadabooks.com and from my website dradebolaadisa.com. See links below.

https://okadabooks.com/book/about/kaleidoscopes/27184

https://www.amazon.co.uk/dp/1546298258/ref=olp_prod uct_details?_encoding=UTF8&me=

#BEINSPIRED

Needing inspiration?

We all need inspiration in our daily lives, every day, sometimes just to get up and go, at other times to keep going.

"#*Beinspired*" is a book that does just that; inspires you.

Writing "#*Beinspired*"

"#*Beinspired*" is a compilation of health topics, inspirational and anecdotal write-ups, poetry, and quotes that I wrote over two years. I have written more about my "#*Beinspired*" writing journey in my book "*How to Write your Book 101: Everyone has a book in them!*".

"#*Beinspired*" is available on Okadabooks.com and from my website dradebolaadisa.com. See the link below.

https://okadabooks.com/search?query=%2523beinspired

References

Atwood, B. (2017, September 12). Tips for Writers: 4 Easy Ways to Back Up Your Writing. Retrieved May 10, 2020, from https://thewritelife.com/losing-your-writing/

Atwood, B. (2020, March 10). Book Editing Basics: 10 Simple Ways to Edit Your Own Book. Retrieved May 12, 2020, from https://thewritelife.com/self-editing-basics/

Copyblogger. (2016) *Copyrighting 101, How to craft compelling copy* (Ebook ed.). (n.d.). Rainmaker Digital, LLC

Delahunty, A., & McDonald, F. (2007). *Oxford pocket school dictionary*. Oxford: Oxford University Press

Fayet, R. (2020, April 23). Book Marketing 101 for Authors (Free Course) • Reedsy. Retrieved May 13, 2020, from https://blog.reedsy.com/learning/courses/marketing/book-marketing-101/

GladReaders. (2018). Different Types or Genres of Books with Examples. Retrieved August 22, 2020, from https://gladreaders.com/types-or-genres-of-books/#biography-autobiography

Hogue, S. (2017, September 05). Developing the Writing Habit. Retrieved August 05, 2020, from https://writingcooperative.com/developing-the-writing-habit-3bbab6c4166f

Lepki, L. (2020, April 23). How to Self-Edit Like A Pro (Free Course) • Reedsy. Retrieved May 12, 2020, from https://blog.reedsy.com/learning/courses/editing/self-edit-like-a-pro/

Sword, H. (2017). *Air & Light & time & space: How successful academics write.* Cambridge, MA: Harvard University Press.

The Mind Tools Content Team, T., Wrote, M., Wrote, V., & Wrote, M. (n.d.). SMART Goals: – How to Make Your Goals Achievable. Retrieved July 30, 2020, from https://www.mindtools.com/pages/article/smart-goals.htm

Yeoh, B. (2017, August 23). Writing Craft. Retrieved May 05, 2020, from https://www.thendobetter.com/arts/2017/8/20/writing-craft

Glossary

Back up

This refers to keeping your manuscript or other write-ups safe beyond just saving it on your chosen medium. Available software include Cloud, Back up, and Dropbox.

Bookpreneur

This is the colloquial term for someone who makes money from the writing, publishing, and marketing of books and all other business opportunities related to books.

Farmacist

This was how my young self, spelt the word *Pharmacist*.

Galley

This is the printer's proof of your book and appears in the form of long columns upon which corrections can be made before your book is made up into pages for the final printing.

Garnishes

This refers to the other aspects of your book which are often considered optional. These include the table of contents, appreciation, dedication, glossary, references, synopsis, and author biography.

Genre

This refers to a specific category of writing: fiction, or non-fiction. It may also describe the writing style or topic. For example, fantasy, romance, memoir, children's literature, adventure, detective, mystery, self-help books, textbooks etc.

ISBN

This refers to the International Standard Book Number.

It is a unique number assigned to each book ever published and no two unique books even by the same publisher or writer should have the same ISBN.

Literary agents

They are paid to represent writers and pitch their written work to traditional book publishers. They can assist in negotiating book contracts and other types of deals including film adaptations and movies.

Manuscript

This refers to any work of an author that has not yet been published.

It may be handwritten or typed.

Medium

This refers to the tangible material which you write on. This may be paper, pages on mobile devices or files and documents on computers. This could also be an audio device.

Pacesetter Book Series:

They are a collection of over a hundred novels written by notable Africans, mostly Nigerians, and published by Macmillan Publishers. The series featured a variety of topics including love, betrayal, tragedy, society ideals and moral themes.

Plagiarising:

This is when you take someone else's ideas, thoughts, expressions, writing or creative work and pass it off as yours.

Proof copy

This is the first copy of your book sent to you by the publisher. It allows you to see the appearance of your published book before anyone else does. You can make any necessary corrections before the final printing stage is completed.

Synopsis

This refers to the summary of your book, which is traditionally placed at the back page so that your target readers can understand what your book is about.

Writer's Block:

This is a condition where a writer cannot write. It may be short or long-lasting.

Write-Up

This is another word for writing, a written account, opinion, review, or an article.

Printed in Great Britain
by Amazon

49742753R00079